The Smart Hat

Maverick
Early Readers

'The Smart Hat'
An original concept by Cath Jones
© Cath Jones

Illustrated by Paul Nicholls

Published by MAVERICK ARTS PUBLISHING LTD

Studio 3A, City Business Centre, 6 Brighton Road,

Horsham, West Sussex, RH13 5BB

© Maverick Arts Publishing Limited July 2017

+44 (0)1403 256941

A CIP catalogue record for this book is available at the British Library.

ISBN 978-1-84886-294-4

www.maverickbooks.co.uk

Blue

This book is rated as: Blue Band (Guided Reading)
This story is decodable at Letters and Sounds Phase 4.

The Smart Hat

by **Cath Jones**

illustrated by **Paul Nicholls**

The Queen's bell was ringing.
Ding-dong.

The Queen took a look in
the big box.

She had such a shock!

The hat said,

"Too-wit-too-woo!"

"This is not my smart hat!"

said the Queen.

The Queen said,

"I need a smart hat *now*."

"I will be a hat," said Owl.

"Just for you!"

The owl sat down

on the Queen's head.

"Wow!" said the crowd.

"Look at the Queen's owl hat!"

"The hat can hoot!" said the crowd.

That night, the Queen took
Owl to the park.

Owl went **zoom** into the dark night!

The next day the Queen felt sad.

But then...

Ding-dong.

...she got a shock!

Quiz

1. That must be _____?
a) My smart hat
b) My smart dress
c) My smart crown

2. What was in the box?
a) A car
b) A brown owl
c) A hat

3. Where does the Queen go with her owl hat?
a) To the zoo
b) To the shops
c) To a park

4. What did the owl do?
a) Hoot
b) Dance
c) Sing

5. The next day the Queen felt...?
a) Sad
b) Happy
c) Angry

Turn over for answers

Book Bands for Guided Reading

The Institute of Education book banding system is a scale of colours that reflects the various levels of reading difficulty. The bands are assigned by taking into account the content, the language style, the layout and phonics.

Maverick Early Readers are a bright, attractive range of books covering the pink to purple bands. All of these books have been book banded for guided reading to the industry standard and edited by a leading educational consultant.

For more titles visit:
www.maverickbooks.co.uk/early-readers

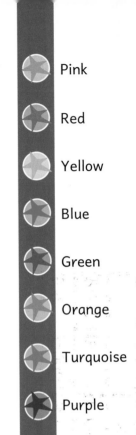

Pink

Red

Yellow

Blue

Green

Orange

Turquoise

Purple

Book Band
Blue

Fast Fox and Slow Snail	978-1-84886-295-1
Mine, Mine, Mine Said the Porcupine	978-1-84886-296-8
The Smart Hat	978-1-84886-294-4
Strictly No Crocs	978-1-84886-240-1
Bibble and the Bubbles	978-1-84886-224-1

Quiz Answers: 1a, 2b, 3c, 4a, 5a